The Hospital

Julie Murray

Abdo

Kids

MY COMMUNITY: PLACES

abdopublishing.com

Published by Abdo Kids, a division of ABDO, PO Box 398166, Minneapolis, Minnesota 55439.
Copyright © 2017 by Abdo Consulting Group, Inc. International copyrights reserved in all countries.
No part of this book may be reproduced in any form without written permission from the publisher.

Printed in the United States of America, North Mankato, Minnesota.

052016

092016

 THIS BOOK CONTAINS
RECYCLED MATERIALS

Photo Credits: iStock, Shutterstock

Production Contributors: Teddy Borth, Jennie Forsberg, Grace Hansen

Design Contributors: Candice Keimig, Dorothy Toth

Cataloging-in-Publication Data

Names: Murray, Julie, author.

Title: The hospital / by Julie Murray.

Description: Minneapolis, MN : Abdo Kids, [2017] | Series: My community: places
    | Includes bibliographical references and index.

Identifiers: LCCN 2015959206 | ISBN 9781680805369 (lib. bdg.) |
    ISBN 9781680805925 (ebook) | ISBN 9781680806489 (Read-to-me ebook)

Subjects: LCSH: Hospitals--Juvenile literature. | Buildings--Juvenile literature.

Classification: DDC 362.11--dc23

LC record available at http://lccn.loc.gov/2015959206

Table of Contents

The Hospital

A hospital is a special place. It is where very sick people get help.

Jo is sick.

The doctor helps her.

Sam broke his arm.

He gets an **x-ray**.

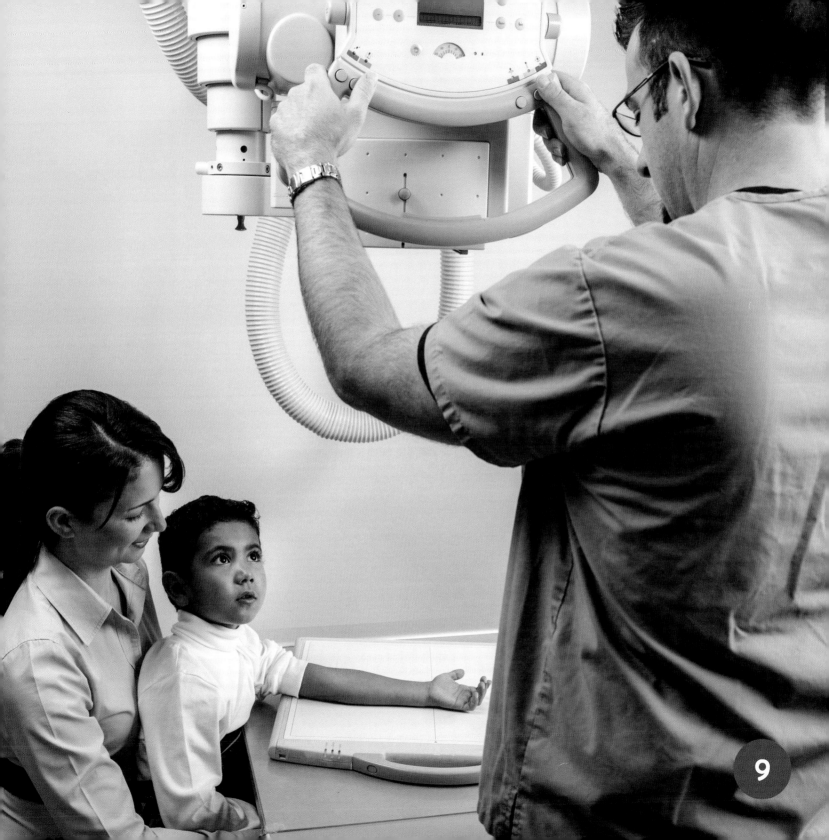

Gabe gets a shot.

This makes him feel better.

Many workers wear masks
and gloves. These keep
germs away.

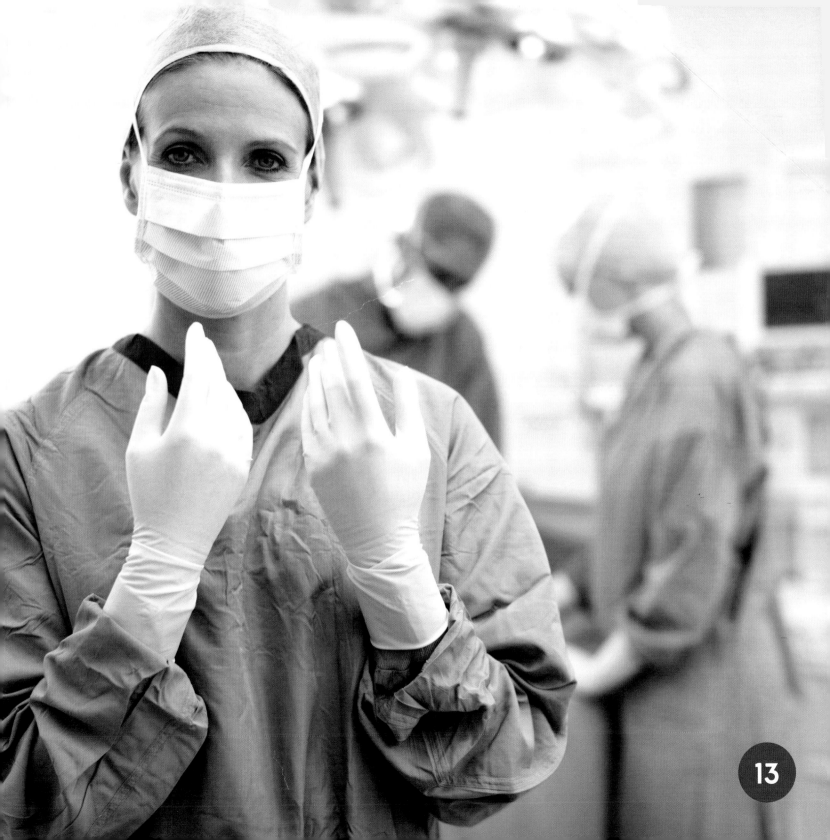

13

Babies are born here, too!

Jackie holds her baby sister.

Ben had **surgery**.

He stays overnight.

He sleeps in a special bed.

Lila visits her grandma.

She is happy to see her!

19

Have you been to a hospital?

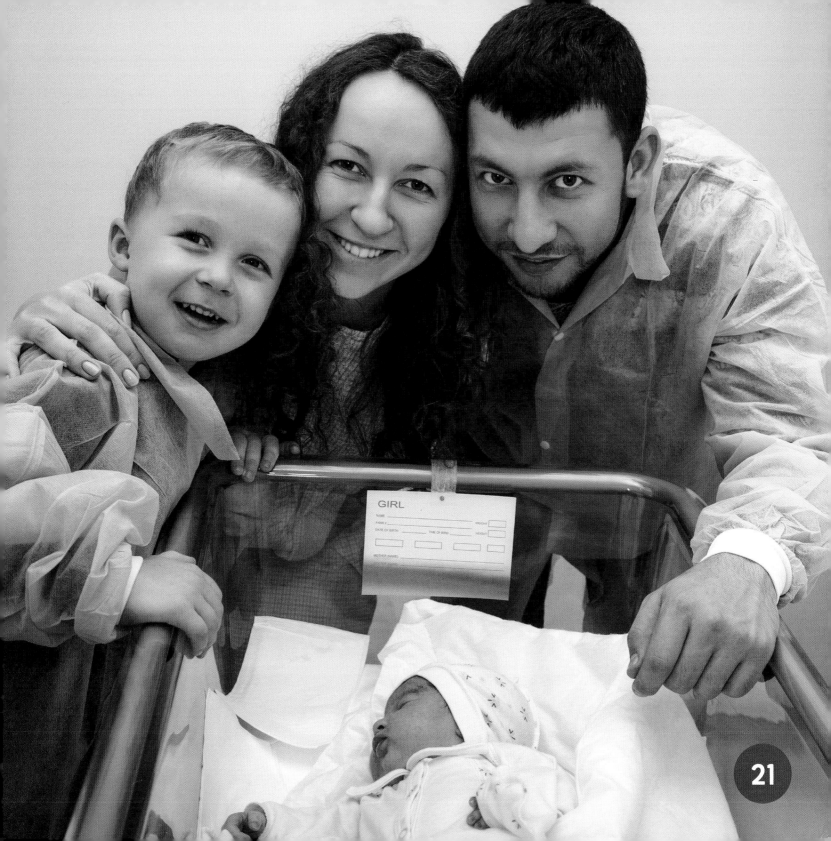

GIRL

NAME

FAMILY

DATE OF BIRTH

TIME OF BIRTH

MOTHER (NAME)

WEIGHT

HEIGHT

21

At the Hospital

doctor

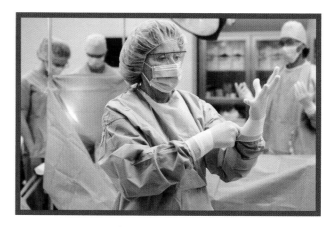

masks and gloves

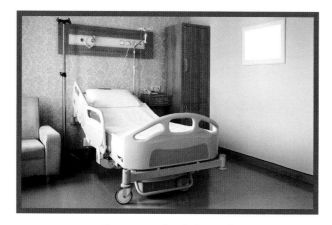

hospital bed

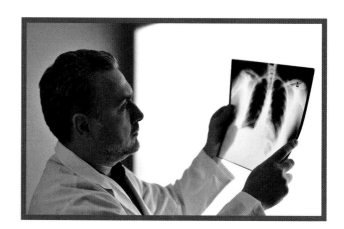

x-ray

Glossary

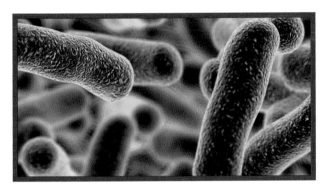

germ
a very small living thing that causes disease.

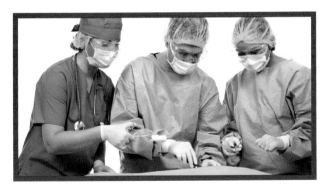

surgery
a medical treatment in which a doctor cuts into someone's body to fix or remove damaged parts.

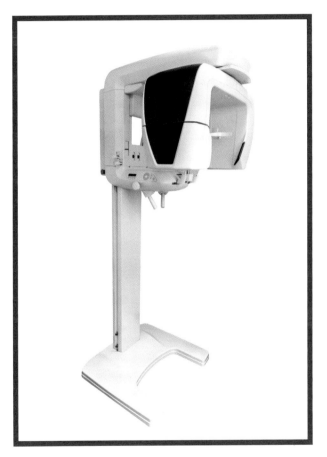

x-ray
examination of a part of the body by taking an x-ray photograph.

Index

abdokids.com

Use this code to log on to abdokids.com and access crafts, games, videos, and more!

Abdo Kids Code:
MTK5369